LIBERATION

of

DISSONANCE

LIBERATION

DISSONANCE

POEMS

BRUCE BOND

Published by Schaffner Press, Inc.

POB 41567

Tucson, Az 85717

Manufactured in the United States

First printing

Cover and interior design: David Ter-Avanesyan/Ter33Design

Library of Congress Control Number: 2021945048

ISBN: 9781639640003

CONTENTS

I.

II.

III.

IV.

PREFACE

To interpret music means: to make music.

—Theodor Adorno, *Quasi una fantasia*

The argument of poetry is only resolved, only laid to rest in the condition of music. In all of his work, Bruce Bond has committed the imagination to music's elusive disciplines and to narratives whelmed by those disciplines into a common humanity. Here, in *Liberation of Dissonance*, Bond's commitment comes to its crisis. As Adorno before him, Bond breaks away from the arcane consolations of Modernism—irony, pastiche, and all such cosmopolitan diversions of the polymath—in order, at last, really to know the condition of music in *this* world, and in this world *now.* Only such knowledge can attend to the sound of "constellations breaking down" ("Verklärte Nacht"). Only such attention, sustained by a sense of the companionship of crisis, can image the unmaking of imagery just as the later Beethoven and the radical Schoenberg scored a liberation of dissonanc from the myth of harmony. There is certainly a stoical quality to Bond's poetry, yet his is a stoicism given to delight in its harrowing liberty.

> *Ever since music has existed, it has always been a protest, however ineffectual, against myth, against a fate which was always the same, and even against death.* (*Quasi una fastasia*)

Dissonance as protest, not against the circumstances of life, but against those easeful inattentions that pretend to affirm life even as they obscure its most vivid realities—this is Bruce Bond's dissonance, deeply instructed by the composers, poets, and jazz masters he joins in crisis. To protest against death, one must acknowledge the reality of death. Empathy must first recognize suffering in its fullness and enigma. And so it is that dissonance becomes the one true and audible sign of life, of real life. How wonderfully apt that Bond should celebrate this recognition in company with men hurrying "to the arms of silhouettes who run at dusk to greet them" ("Grodek"). The poet embraces shadows, having at last accomplished the fellowship of shadows, thus giving them flesh.

> *Music, contracted to a moment, is true as an eruption of negative experience. It touches on real suffering.*
> (Adorno, *Philosophy of New Music*)

I can think of no other word for this fellowship than "soul". But soul is never free for the asking. (Perhaps that is why the word has, once again, gone out of fashion.) It must be won by strict attention, by the penitence that always follows upon strict attention, and by the empathy that liberates dissonance at the end of all. As Bond declares in his poem "Beethoven", "There is no mistake without the innocence that makes it. Forgive me. I know. A boy/is weeping at the keys." The condition of music is human, disciplined away from mythology by the dissonance of one child weeping. The soul is the child.

—Donald Revell

I

We have actually three dimensions in music: horizontal, vertical, and dynamic swelling or decreasing. I shall add a fourth, sound projection—that feeling that sound is leaving us with no hope of being reflected back, a feeling akin to that aroused by beams of light sent forth by a powerful searchlight.

—Edgard Varèse, "The Liberation of Sound"

VERKLÄRTE NACHT

The dawn of the age is an old tune just barely in d minor.
You can go there, listen, hear what Arnold Schoenberg heard

as he walked the block at midnight composing in his head.
You can turn the page scarred with accidentals and feel the tonal

constellations breaking down: stars pulled from one another,
night from day, day from days before, and, behind the system,

the beauty of the clear black glass. But the system remains.
It gives blood to the corpus, a pulsing structure to the blood.

To listen is to know half the music is never there, as the whole
of a language lies elsewhere in an act of speech, or the screen

lies low in exile, beyond the movie, invisible, blind, and nothing
comes to light without it. A glow of promise gives each detail

the darkness of an inner life. Without which mass has no gravity,
starlight no contingency, no fiery nature, the warm slash chord

no sternum to divide. The double-flatted and refused, they call
to the transfixed who hear less the indictment of a practice

than a facelift to its gods. Progress as numbed, sliced, needled,
stitched. By angel of accident or grace, the unexpected aberration

spreads to breed a culture of permission. A Mesmer, a Freud,
a lust, an André Breton, an automatic method. They are in there

if you listen, slit open by the long nocturnal scalpel of the strings.
Clarity is never so clear as imagined. But the graves are opening.

Mist rising. A newly sharped voice-leading presses deeper into flesh.
Schoenberg was in love, and in the heaven of a season

some call cloudy, others clear, he read a poem about a woman,
shy, ashamed, pregnant by someone other than her lover.

But the lover forgives her, and so this arc of stars across
the reaches of d-minor, these bone-inflected wings against

the staves. Schoenberg was in love and soon would marry.
Soon the wilderness of culture would get more poisonous.

To every birth, the pain that leads an infant to its refuge,
the exile to a home. If the poem made audible its anthem

of forgiveness, it needed what forgiveness needs.
Not amnesia but resistance. It needed to pull the thread

of tension from *this* violin, *that* transgression. To recall
just so much. Never more. After all, there was a child

on the way, a room to prepare. There was a new life now,
in whom the cry of nights to come opened to admit him.

LAMELLA

Beneath the waver of the dorsal fin lie the blood-shades
of lamellae, their skin so close to the vein they breathe,

filter, gather, flex, set down in loose and frangible parallels
you find in gills of mushrooms, clams, and concertinas.

Wave after wave, the tissues of the water breathers
conceal what they reveal, according to their vital rhythm.

Fins that breathe flit this way, that, in the give and take
of panic and lust and tropical surge from no one place.

To every fish, flesh, nightmare, and song: a private opening
and the name it bears. Let us call it *tomorrow* or *lament,*

the heart of my volition. To every want the one who wants,
chosen, given, taken in. To every bride, the lamellae

of the sugar and sleeve. Layers of lace that advertise
the power of enclosure, how, in some siege of arrival,

a white interior lathers the shore. Somewhere downwind
the music at the altar, both bride and gown take a shape.

One part surge, another spray. One part the urging
of the processional march. A woman wets the mouthpiece

of her oboe, blows, adjusts the angle with her fingers.
She understands the value of a quality double-reed,

the thin resilient tip that, when sounded, vanishes from view.
The better lamellae take time. The better harvest

from cane fields of southern France. First the cut,
the cure, the second shape and then, by laser-beam, a third,

and finally the carve of a craftsman who will go nameless.
Now we are coming to the passage reminiscent of a fish.

We are speaking a loose-limbed language as it swims
the caverns, in the ear, out the mouth, encircling the future

groom, asleep, and the body of his bride beside him, almost
there. Our darkness breathes more deeply in the dark.

Somewhere a fly taps the window and dies. Night's web
flutters. A mushroom slips the bricks of the drive. It wants

in, and out, and neither, revealed and concealed as childhood
is, and music will be, and all we lost, seek, and never find.

We are coming to the passage reminiscent of a tune
though we cannot know just what or where. When I was a boy,

my skin was so thin I spent most days alone. I wandered
the yard and was its lord, its terror, its scared apprentice.

Mostly I was no one. I was just that transparent, that adrift.
Beneath the brim of the cap, the mushroom's papery fan

broke to pieces at my touch. It crumpled the way bodies do
beneath a shared diagnosis. I thought I killed the pattern in

my hand, but what I held were spores. Beneath the umbrella
of a new cloud, what I felt was the first light breath of rain.

GRÓDEK

When the smoke cleared and took with it the sirens
          and the uniforms strung across our sofas,

what remained were rivers, mist, whisper as a habit,
          red dawn in the eyes of the sleep deprived.

In the brush, here and there, beside the highway,
          the revenant scent of metal and decay.

The good news was the soldiers were returning.
          And you could find them. You could see them

walk the paths and asylums of the southern valley.
          It was here Georg Trakl—the pharmacist, writer,

depressive, friend—arrived to administer council,
          cocaine, whatever distillate or talk, to steward

efforts of recovery in whom he had so little faith.
          Any wonder his affinity for music, the language

of a faith without a language, a doctrine, a God.
    Only the fog that jewels the woods at night,

a bone-white moon driven down the throats
    of the addled like a pill. Less to eviscerate

a past than to let it breathe, to give it a little something
    for the pain. Suffering has a local address.

It will tell you. It has its Gródeks whose blood is less
    corrosive, invasive to the eye, laid in the river.

Georg Trakl was a generous man. And if cocaine
    and the flask of ether came off his shelf too often,

if the man's face took on, in time, the pallor of ice,
    do not say he failed his calling. Only that he turned

from one world among the many, the way a forest
    turns to shadow, or the shadows to men, men

to the arms of silhouettes who run at dusk to meet them.

WOLVES

The song called "Lonely Woman" has no woman in it,
no loneliness as pure as we imagine, no language save

the trumpet and the sax who braid between them one
great rope, charmed, rising, and yes, the bass and drum,

that steady ground to leverage something of another
earth, its fortunate burden, its upward wish. Here I am,

says *the devil's tone,* as ancient churches called it,
as if the ear possessed the power to resist, to keep hell out

of paradise for good. Ask the woman, she will tell you.
Take any octave and crack it, and there she is, silent, still.

Today I was listening to Ornette Coleman. It was 1959.
The measures were not free. They were music. Take

any word and crack it, and a breath comes out, released.
Released, we say, and then we hear our world on the other side.

Heaven, too, longs to be inclusive, flush with the dissonant
adventure that, in another era, frightened and confused.

What woman, trapped in lyric space, would not become
more vital to a stranger. She longs as Ornette Coleman did

when he played his plastic sax. He found it in a pawnshop.
It was all that he could afford. And though at first he did

not like it, he grew fond of it. The feather-weight shaft,
the brittle voice. How strong it was, and is. This will to connect.

Long ago I heard the sound of two wolves across a valley.
No grid of lights. No mother in the dark of the cradle.

Only earth. The exhumation of some sweet scent there.
It sounded honeyed at first, the binding of the voices,

the way they bleed like sirens into echoes, echoes
into the silence to come. And then I heard in each

the rift. The radiance, the teeth, the anonymity,
the glory. And I would not take its cry to heart for years.

BELLS

Wind with barely a world in its path makes no sound.
And then the banner lifts and flutters. The one hand claps.

Bronze comes invisibly to life, and the startled temple
mourns the missing hand. Who here is not a child of bells.

They blow to song the abstracts of men through the open
garret. Who is it now, I wonder. And the bells turn back

to stone. Today I watched a movie of the killing. I thought,
perhaps, it would make me wise, responsive, or, in excited

horror, prone to see suspicion blown into a monster. I
am just one hand after all. A man is there. I do know this.

Bones of light, flesh of shadow, and as the gun goes off,
the wind of the known trajectory blows an abstract of men

through the open lesion. Who here is not a child.
Fire moves through broken windows and the figures in

a riot, and the names get taken down or lost. Night burns.
Embers graze the eye, but the movie does not change.

Characters are cast, in bronze this time, committed, bound
to mistakes they made or suffered or deepened by neglect.

Those who walk the tear gas go unseen. Some are pulled
aside, questioned, searched, and never found. Others

hang in the heart of the bayou like bells, and no one hears.
Some walk the pathless walk of bronze in the tower.

Forward and back, the stride of the breath and the broom
and the hasp of the flag beaten into wind and cinders.

However singular the bullet and path of light, the door
in the body swings both ways. In. And farther in.

The banner claps the air, and somewhere men prepare
the body for the viewing. Flowers release their ghost.

Overhead you hear the silence on which a music lies.
It is template-hard, cold, steady as the embalmer's table.

Say the widow is the one hand, her open bed the other.
The bronze that strikes her from her nightmare is the bell.

I have felt my own music overfill the vessel of the killer.
Whatever the misconception, it is looking for another:

a word to strike, a mirror, a wall. And now the movie
has come down offline. The children are sequestered.

The gun-metal river goes cold. Wind with barely a world
in its path fills and empties the needles of the valley.

Where there is a breath, there is an obstacle in its path.
America touches no one in particular and so a little of all.

It cracks as men in grief and office do. Every bell is
two bells, one silent, the other made of words that so miss

the world, they whisper, *look.* They break us open, and then,
in tired voices, break, so full of promise, they cannot find us.

FOR TIM WHOM NONE CAN FIND

The day he pulled the cord on Carlos and the bass
vanished, when we on stage felt the missed

connection, we knew something spoke to Tim
that had no Carlos in it, a voice beyond words,

though it came between us all that day, and we
went our broken ways. So little left. So much,

it seems, that's better said as silence, and isn't
that the problem. Days when the abscessed

dejection takes us by surprise. How could I
know a part of him was longing to be lanced.

Whatever grief he felt when his father died,
Tim put it, like an animal, down. He inhaled

the ash of his inheritance in coke. Not much,
but pure, uncut. And then, he left. I tried,

but I could not find him; no one can, we say,
meaning none we know. I keep losing him

each time I play his blowout in my head.
His ghost, in me, sings alone, as notes must be

to be a part and so, in vanishing, a music.
Still I want to know. I search online. I scroll

self-studied galleries of Tims in whom
I hear the countdown to a flash. I hear my own.

I see whatever sunk that day the lower
registers went silent, when Carlos looked at me,

helpless, and I said, *I quit,* and my Vibrolux
hummed a numb drone, as each of us unplugged.

WOZZECK

Even the toneless whisper finds its cradle, its home,
let alone the marginal harmony so central to our story,

even the clouds as they gather water, the sun the better
reasons to lie down. Which is when our hero, Wozzeck,

binding sticks in no key in particular, tells his friend,
All is still, as if the world died. But his friend is elsewhere,

as music is, however near. If the composer saw his own
experience here, in those who would not, could not, listen,

what you hear are sticks on fire. What you see is a man
whose shadow falls into the shadows of distant towers.

What you recall is bodies falling into one anonymous grave.
The funeral hymn decomposes into military cadence.

Sad figures of the leaves and branches have lost their silhouette.
But the shadows are out there somewhere. The silence

of friends turns to something as it turns. In the early phases
of refusal, the sticks that the fascist gathers are men.

The physician deepens his experiments into the poor.
His instruments work a little closer, and the heart recoils.

And the whole cast is singing now in no one key.
One person's symptom is another's prophecy. Another's science

dreams of reputation and moves men from machine to machine,
the music of the living from passacaglia to chorale.

All of us are building toward a clearer, more corrosive
bewilderment. The world has not died. It just acts that way.

And Wozzeck is its orphan, before he is our monster.
He is the wounded child he was, before he makes an orphan

of his son. We who watch, we can see it coming. However
drugged. We who take our place in the darker portion

of the house, if we know anything, we know something
of the dark, how deep the madness cuts, what it takes

when it takes its life. But the boy—Wozzeck's son—is
another matter. And so he stares into the space off-stage

the other boys abandon. He is unaware his parents have died,
and though the image he makes, transfixed by children's

voices in the distance, makes us wonder, a part of us wants
to spare him, to wrap his eye in tissues for the journey.

Call it merciful. To arrive again at no one key and think of it
as home. Call it the odd unlikely reason why we come.

And for weeks we will see ourselves there. We return.
To bury deep in him our memory: our flowers and our sword.

LORCA

You hear it best where the key turns minor
          and enters a field you did not know was there,

but it was always there, you think, this star,
          day or night, this jewel in the mine,

always a wilderness that pulls from earth
          its slow dark architectural progress.

A boat slips beneath the harbor bridge
          a letter that says, by the time you get this,

I will be gone. And yet you read there
          some tender argument: know that I am

thinking of you. Or: please, be not afraid.
          The mere mention of fear sounds its own

danger, alone in the harbor, flagged in mist.
          Wherever music goes farthest, deepest,

you hear the speaker trapped inside it,
    longing to be clear. And it is that failure,

that is clearest, the hesitant strength,
    hope and its refusals, that phrase the matter.

It is the need to be there, among the lost,
    that carves the marble of all things here.

MEASURE

1.

The world's first drum was nothing we would call
a drum, nothing, that is, until we heard it,

the heartwood gutted by obsidian, or knives,
or fire, or the slow sure violence of time

driven through the chamber. To hear it now,
the hollow core and the force that strikes it,

to give the vessel its signature timbre,
its *live* sound, and feel that sound decay,

we need a little of the spirit that found
us, making something out of nothing,

as kids do and certain habits of unease.
We need a silence to displace, a past

to bleed through, as the unheard in the heard,
or wounds that redden the cloth that binds them.

2.

It skins them, like a drum. We are born out
of this, our world, but also *into* it.

Out of the wilderness, the sound of drums.
Out of nothing a child's choice to listen.

Out of the dark, the voice that says, what
I really need is time. I learned to hurry

when my steps were smaller than the others'.
I leaned a step ahead of my body,

and my father stopped, waited, and still
I never arrived. Out of nothing, the gallop,

the fist, the thunder, the language saying, *now, now,*
at intervals that measured not time alone,

but our path in it, our sense of *please God, not*
yet, and *remember, love,* and *sometime soon.*

3.

Our drums keep time, we say, but we know better.
We know music as neither time

nor its keeper, neither mastery nor dread.
No bridling of the scarred behemoth,

no crumpling of winter widows into streams.
It is a language for no language, a pulse

beneath the skin of words, the compulsory
insistence of a chisel breaking stone.

What music makes, it unmakes. It moves, we move.
Hair slips from its ribbons. And the head

that rocks in its cradle has a child in it,
slipping off to where the measures end,

ocean begins. In the gutted body
we leave behind, the breathing of the shore.

4.

Long ago suns rose and fell in the great
clock of skies that would never fall,

the great phonograph with its axis,
its great observers who measured every move.

The music of the spheres was, for them,
a sphere. The sympathetic shiver from star

to star gave off the aura of one star,
one pulsing zero in a tally of debts.

The more the great observers measured the more
they fell asleep facedown on their charts.

For they were believers and so possessed
and followed a ghost of song that believes

nothing, and is no one, and pours its cup
of stars each night into a frozen sea.

5.

The great observers were the first to admit.
They heard no tune. Because they always heard it.

Music came, if it came, in the flesh of an idea,
a ghost, a mostly hollow place, lost

as any paradise and those we leave there.
So it is with interiors that have no skin,

no meat, no interior. This *god,* this *O,*
who has no center, no wall of stars to knock,

no door to leave the pilgrim of our bones.
I have been to a house like that. I stood

to sing in an old stone church, to offer
hymns whose words return because I sang them.

Beside me, the father who never talked
of what we sang to whom, wherever, and why.

6.

But there he was, faithful as a watch,
the practical half singing to the other.

We sang together, badly, the hidden valves
and bellows of our bodies joined in time.

I never saw him take the invisible
as gospel, but more as one takes a breath,

a moment, a matter more lightly, and then,
invisibly, to change the conversation.

What I do know is our suns continued
to rise and fall and the morning to pour

its pitcher of light. *Give us this day,* we said
as we were told, as those before us said

and so bore the same gold torch across
the threshold of their passing. It got old.

7.

Forgotten. And now and then new again.
The world's first drum was the animal heart.

It must have known something we did not,
that a body needs a suitcase with a sea

inside. It needs to carry ashore the salt
and tide of some obscurity it crawled from.

It needs blood and closure and some time
in the wilderness. Some place to hide.

The world's first instrument was time. Then
the ghost stepping out of the body

and in and out again, the ocean pulse
that says, the infinite is coming and then

it never does. When my father died,
he stopped cold. Like a watch. He waited.

8.

Most of what I touch is missing. So says
the science of small things, child steps,

particle shards, whose tally comes up short.
Most of what a mind touches is lost

the moment that we reach it. When I was small,
I nearly drowned. Night after night

God's ocean beats its measures in the dark.
It's still there. The hammer as the father

of the nail. Lightening a stride before the thunder.
For all I know, the world's first voice was wind

as atoms are and hearts when you break them.
Everywhere you look, the whirr of small fears

we do not hear because we always hear them.
We who were born of violence. None recalls.

9.

These days the greater measure of rhythm
    is silence; of language, air; of the day to day,

the passing expectation. There is a note
    of panic in the higher resonance of praise,

a quiet violence in the joy that breaks.
    And the drummer, in the heated sections,

sends a gallop through the wilderness.
    Most of what I know I forget. I hear it,

the ghost of it, in this. I hear the father
    I knew in one I never will. A believer

then and so a head full of chaos laid down
    in Eden like a child. The greater measure

of flesh is blood turned muscle that beats the door
    it cannot open. And then, at rest, it does.

III

It's always night, or we wouldn't need light.

—Thelonious Monk

THE OCTAVES

If the river star mirrors a higher origin, a clearer
smaller version whose water is the still air,

what I see is the light of the emptiness between them
and time that passes through. What I hear

is the arrow of a sharper thing in the ripple
of the target, halos pulsing from the wound.

And there, in the low violas, the figure borrowed,
stolen, given back, and in the measure after,

the moaning of ships and bridges of the harbor.
Cranes bow down to the shoreline docks.

Oil from the gulf. Refuse on the barges.
Cities move. They must. They live to float

the nameless gift or burden across the frets
of shade. Traffic merges suicidal into traffic,

and because this dissonant world is our only child,
we do the best we can. *To resolve,*

says the older language, is *to break.* I want
to say life was simpler as a child, but the child

is not so sure. *To resolve, to reduce, to make*
the memorial resolution measured and small.

Or grind as clocks grind time into miniscule bells,
and the hour's first overtone is an older number.

Of all the stretches on the fingerboard, the octave
most reveals our intonation. It breaks us in.

And the child hears her mother at the door say,
A little flat, and so grows anxious with this note,

that, and the emptiness between them. Long ago
to resolve was *to loosen* and later *to hold,*

and now the girl is a woman, and the stage a far cry
from the practice room, its dreary repetitions.

Still she is resolved, and so she crosses over.
Bells set loose a flock around the steeple.

Still she is afraid, and still she moves. She must.
She and the long unlovely hours drawn closer

to perfection. I love discord as I love problems.
The ones you solve and un-solve, the slipknots

of their waves. Time, the unsolvable, drives
the instrument that makes an ocean possible

to bear. I love the strollers on the bridges who scan
the harbor in search of what, they do not

know, some hidden principle of waves perhaps,
its necessity, its yield, its readiness to surprise.

Beneath the octaves of the high curve, they look.
They smoke. They vanish. The smolder

that lifts from oceans in the morning says,
remember. But what *this* says remains unclear.

Truth is, the dissonance of fog at dawn breaks
to pieces when you touch it. Last night comes

undone, and you lift it to your ear and listen.
You come not close but close enough to talk.

Ask the violinist. She too talks to the doll

of her hands, her mother's child. She knows.

Sometimes the kinder, better dialogue is song,

and perfect kids are the first to crumble.

Perfect, from the Latin, *perfectus, complete,*

as circles are, and the other hollow objects.

The O of emptiness that has no home in nature.

Seasons, stars, the open target of the gaze:

the greater our exile, the smoother the curve

of contour and path, the falling in the distance.

The more sublime the steel that plants its feet

in the harbor, the burdens slipped below.

The moaning of ships is never long for the world.

A little flat, says the mother. She is only human.

Long ago I stumbled at my mother's funeral

over a line in the eulogy, and it moved some.

Others did not notice. Every song was two songs.

One of which I heard. I was fragile as an angel

and could not write. For those who come
to negotiate, to wash: a little power washes back.

A little power washes out. The vaulted fifths
of the plainchant and cathedral are impersonal.

I love that, as I love the enormity of spaces that make
me and these losses small. If you play

a dissonance again, it loses some of its edge, the metal
of its obligation. It tears free of the child

but never free of us. If you chart the physics of nerves
and expectations, the particles keep changing.

With them, the boundaries of what we kill, forgive,
shelter and enthrall. I was not simple as a child.

I was as broken as an angel. I opened each box
of smoke and so grew unburdened and confused.

A little power washed out, a little power wandered in.
The girl at the violin says, *If you forgive yourself*

enough, it is not you alone. If you stand backstage,
you can feel the bodies breathe, the dark breath

in the fading voices. If you take your place,
    you take something of the empty circle with you.

Something of the child and the mother she is losing.
    If you close your eyes. And then. The music.

WAVE

The voice on the radio says, I do not know music,
but I know what I like. Or was it, I like what I know.

Either way I understand. Though it seems that must be half
a man talking, the other half the radio we talk over,

and a friend drops by to say this morning he put his cat
to sleep, and I say I know what that is like, and half

the talk is bread that must be broken, the other the long
solitude you hear in a broke-down church. My friend says,

he told his cat he was sorry to see her go, and the cat replied,
But I am here. And as we talk, the radio wonders,

What is the use of me. Is there something in the music
of questions that pull us from bed and just keep rising.

Something in song's continuous farewell that whispers,
I am sorry. And the upward eye's reply, *But I am here.*

SYRINX

Of all the songbirds, the nightingale wanders least in body,
most in song, the inventions so prodigious who is to say

what varies what, where a theme ends, variation begins.
Those who read the whole arrangement puzzle over why.

From a disarray of branches: the new species, breeds,
and finely painted bugs to eat them. Of all the canaries,

the brightest prospects ruffle the most delighted feathers.
The syrinx in their throats is double-pitched, broken

at the brachial divide where the labia flutter a sound so sweet
it cuts a bird in two. There is a trick I play. I invent

a vernacular to thread the pearls of a genus on one long
string, the many women and men on one long breath.

With every name, a pierce. Then the other trick: the one
becomes one alone, and that too draws a sigh of relief.

The depressive rises from bed. *Dawn* has never been *this* dawn.
Welcome to the world, it says, so impenetrable, ineffable,

calm, no one answers, no one calls. Why is there everything
instead of one thing, one ocean inside these oceans of light.

Long ago I watched my mother sleep and never wake.
What if it is nothing, she asked me, eyes wide, the night before.

And I had no answer. I said, *Be calm. You're fine.* Then I
read her a poem by a man who loved the cows, the map-

like patterns on their backs, the chaos that bears testament
to the glory of all. *Praise,* he said, *for the thread that binds*

the many breeds of elephant and flu, the inarticulate cry,
the carnivorous bloom. To the red-throated warbler, praise,

and the song that breaks a warbler open, the pruning
shears as manic as the rose. For the world has fallen

from a high place and shattered gardens over earth
And the scattered pieces need each other to be seen.

They need to be named, loved, then unnamed to be seen
once more. Of all the songs, the wordless variations

travel farthest, across the graves of oceans, breakers,

shores; *Praise the light,* they say, *that needs a place to fall.*

SIREN

Then the captain dipped his hand into a jar
of wax, held it up to his crew, and said, *Use this,*

and though it bore a likeness to our own flesh,
he dropped it back in the vessel with the thud

of meat or some such burden, wiped his hand
on a goatskin, and you probably know the rest.

It did the trick. The last thing the sailors heard
was an order to go silent. And so they ignored

the gestures of a man obsessed, lashed to the mast.
They did not fret cautionary tales of the drowned

expeditions, the men lost to a madness, the news
that survived. We take these stories, if we do,

on faith, because there is a heavier fog on the horizon.
There is a destination whose song could be your last

confession. Always a jut of rocks between a sailor
and his summons. A slash in the water to open

the choir and a mast to serve as anchor. So why risk
the straits whose casualties say nothing. Was it

nothing he wanted, some great unburdened harvest
of journey, some lip of foam against the shore.

Was it the prospect of the small death that unbuckled
his shield. The waves were lovely when he suffered.

And for a time afterwards, he thought of nothing else.
He walked the deck among the others and yet

a step away. His mind felt larger, as if experience alone
were understanding. But just what he knew

he did not know. And for years, he woke in the dark
and heard not music but the silence after, the path

it took, far from shore, the fog that walked the broken water.

CRY

When he was no one to an island nation,
he loved the turn in a dime-store novel

when aliens descend in their starships
to teach us, the wounded, how to live.

There is another world, and it is here
he practiced his instrument till dawn,

and his fingers bled. If music talked,
it made an argument with powerful men

an anthem, a proud sound to soften
the blow of a father's hand. He relished

that, not the hand, but the blossom
of a Fender Twin pushed to saturation.

To every bend, a body leaned against
the wind. If the siren of higher resonance

took the fundamental over, it was not
pain as he had known it. Not pain alone.

If a Cry Baby mouthed the story of a boy,
what we hear is the end of the story.

Already the ear has grown more liberal
with dissonance. A terrible payload falls.

In the middle of a hymn to the new republic,
it whistles, shreds. There is another world

that ends. Trash is gathered. Traffic flows.
But for a mesmerized few, one last song,

where the man with a Strat pulls a howl
from his chamber, and the shoeless hunt for shoes.

BODY

In the shadows of a lost home, a bird-yellow

record machine spins a nameless tune.

Its name is somewhere. I know. But for me,

the needle grinds a shroud around its voices,

and I miss, as a boy, the worn-out shield

about the power cord until, that is, I grasp it.

And why not. I know so little of wires, shielded

or unshielded, how they long to connect.

Power can lock your grip, in awe of a body

you have no power over. I am one child still

with a child's toy, a child's canary, so my first shock's

a puzzle, a tickle; my second a wound.

I am one part boy, another machine, another a song

that leaves and just keeps leaving,

and my mother does not hear it. Only the cry
    I make before I know it was I who made it.

I open my mouth, and pain falls out, and still
    the shock continues. I want to say a neighbor

girl sits close by though I do not know her name.
    I know I alone touch the broken part,

and unsure if I find pleasure there, I touch again.
    I alone go in. I could play you more.

I could let the needle dig a little deeper.
    But as the lattice of shade across us tells you,

I do not know their names, only *my* names,
    how I summon them, how I, that day, become

more a body and less the one who understands it.
    The way things work gets more dark,

more warm to the touch and faceless farther in.
    If I touch the wire again, I ground a terror

in the singing machine, and a part of me must
    like it. A part of me completes the circuit

in a mother's general unease. If this is power,
    it is not mine. It is the tale my body tells me.

It makes me. It says, *Remember the bird*
    you startled when you cried. And real or not,

I do. I want to say the neighbor girl is terrified.
    I want to place her in the matrix of names

and needles. But when I look up, she is not there.
    I ask the shadow, the sky. I ask the tune.

I ask the emptiness, but it does not answer.
    It does not hear. And then, in shock, it does.

PHOENIX

Herman Blount, aka *Sonny,* aka the new man *Sun Ra,*
took the name of a god and star older than his nation.

Both man and name will tell you, his nation is not his.
It is a scaffolding of words in which a boy is raised.

Slaves take names and sacks of ivory on their backs.
When Sun was young, he suffered his share. Ropes

in the trees of Alabama. The crack in the branches
where they cut the body down. What we know we know

as dead. But add, for him, the chronic shame, the long
ache and inflammation of his undescended manhood.

If he woke in pain, he played a little music, a solo
on his horn, and fell asleep again. Call him touched

by angel or fire. Or disgrace. Whatever the source,
a vision came to him. Whatever the fiat or symptom,

he visited the planet Saturn in a dream and thereby forged
a covenant with an alien race. Imagine the disorder.

It is coming, he thought, the revolution. And he was born
to write its anthem. If the demigods slipped him letters,

news from an undisclosed location—call it Harlem
or Giza or ancient Athens—if they gave his ache a calling

or distraction, then God's speed. *Dear Sun,* they said,
I am counting on you. Dear Sun, he echoed. And you

can hear it in the synth and cymbal of his sci-fi group,
his *arkestra,* the beast and phoenix of the reeds, the lamb

of the silver, the lions of the drums. In the dervish, you
can see the sun-gold threads of the high-legged dancers.

Of all the gods of dismantlement, fire is the father.
Forger of the hatchet and the sax, the latch of the snare,

the spur, bronze embossments of the warrior's shield.
Forger of the imagery there you hear about in myths,

and the parts gone silent. Rope in the branches.
Genitalia on a pike. Herman Blount was dead.

And he kept rising with the smoke and the falsified
reports and the goddess of beauty in a lather,

born of the severed pride from the last king here.
Herman Blount was rising with the skin and stench

of the master's brand, rising and falling in the fires
of Los Angeles. And the west turned red, riotous

with canisters of gas. Local businesses broke in flames
for they were never local enough. Sunny was dead,

and a new man woke inside his nerves and problems.
A new insomniac walked to the kitchen, spun a record

of Cecil Taylor, the furious, and grew, by grace,
exhausted. He knew. The world in deepest exile walks

the coldest path. It wears a raiment cut from the sun.
And when it moves, the system trembles. Like a body

in bare ecstasy or pain. And the pharaohs hear it.
And the horn. And the dancers shiver their bracelets of fire.

THE THROAT SINGERS OF TUVA

To harmonize with a waterfall, you must listen
to the river as many, and none, and give

to each a voice. You must hear in each
the glacier of its origin, the mirror and the sun

that turns the lock of it, the name of one
thing turning to another, to the weeping

of the first small transformation—what we call,
for want of words, the first. To harmonize

with the great white noise, you must hear
in it the long grey streak of estuary silt

days from here, the clash that is a river's
ruin and rebirth. To sing the sea to shreds,

you must turn as oceans turn their pages
to the shore, calling to mind the cascades

of jailbreak and avalanche and certain
cooling systems and you, a child of the child

you were, who watched your mother
break down in her dotage. Do not call it

cutting edge. Call it a field. Call the birds
of the clearing with their needles and threads,

their wings that close a phantom fabric.
Call the flocks that turn to rivers and fade

across the skyline. To raise the dead,
you must break pitch as they broke once

and bones and pods and scared confessors
or winds across the rocks of the tundra

or the cry of the camel who lost her calf.
Grave, we say, when we talk of voices born

low, and when they rise, they drag a little
of the body with them. The deep red part.

To speak in grief you must become a little
 speechless. To harmonize is to divide.

Listener and singer and, nights like this,
 chisels of rain, they make the cliffs of Tuva

smooth as mirrors. If you hold a finger up,
 you feel a breeze, what the grasses feel,

the stones whose voices make them small,
 the weather large, and thus included.

To join the choir you must walk away, lose
 your bearings. Isn't that what you wanted.

To widen the eye of the pool at the bottom.
 To drop your burden like a coin of light

that cannot quite go through. The window
 of a younger voice is never so transparent

as remembered. The timbre of it changes
 because you change. It crinkles like a face

in the fire. You have heard the explanations,
 the name of the *river* that never steps

in the same breath twice, and you are learning
to survive. The incantations have come

to tell you the human throat is fathomless.
And if it rises, if the great well stands before us,

who are we to resist. If the white erasure
comes crashing through, what is any voice

that it would tear the echo from its source,
the trauma of descent from the gathering mist.

IV

As the ear becomes acclimatized to a sonority within a particular context, the sonority will gradually become 'emancipated' from that context and seek a new one.

—Arnold Schoenberg, "Opinion or Insight"

BEETHOVEN

In a rumored portrait sketched by his neighbors,
Ludwig as a boy is weeping at the clavier.

He is standing on a footstool to reach the keys
where a father passes down the cruelty of perfection.

The music is in there, if you look hard, head
bowed, heavy as a lantern by a still night lake.

The cracks in the face of the ivories make
what we do not play a dark interior, a child

in a well, an eye in the eye-white context of snow.
In a rumored portrait, the clock forever chips

the rock in its path. Where this all begins—
the path, the dread, the music—is undisclosed,

as early childhood is, and before that, the practice
of switches and stung hands passed from fathers

to sons to those the songs we play imagine.
There is no mistake without the innocence

that makes it. Forgive me. I know. A boy
is weeping at the keys. His chords are gloves

he slips through into winter ice that jewels
the bitter angels of the field. Forgive me, winter,

whose cruelty is snow, whose absolution is
more snow. Forgive me, father of the man

whose only children are songs, portraits, drifts
drawn through the perfect stillness of our hands.

Winter cannot hear you. It is an emperor one
moment, and then the field behind the portrait.

The field behind the field. *I am not difficult,*
the composer said. *Do not remember me that way.*

Remember me driven from home, abandoned
here in the distance where we, in silence, meet.

And you, my beloved, imagine a snow of letters
falling into snow, words that enter the glove

of breath in December. Every winter is one now,

every visible whisper I never felt, each distant

promise in the season whose anger is a child.

No beginning without the nameless precedent

stumbling in a field. A future, that, as music,

never quite arrives. And the phrase before it

never leaves. Thus: this joy in praise of a joy

expected, mythologized, lost as words to a child

at the keys, head bowed above the shattered plaster.

Somewhere between the boy and the mask lifted

from his face at the end, the middle of a journey

improvised long hours at the instrument and gleaned

at best a sketch we call an opus, a body, a work.

Mostly it is invisible. This flesh. Each vital part

unreal to us until, that is, it fails. But sometimes

you can hear it: the flesh with its obscure interior

stepping into the sonata, mourning the silence

at either end. And our name for non-disclosure,

imperfectly, is *soul.* It is the deeper red of blood

          before the harvest, before it saves another

or kills you, or both, before one boy's grief

          became the reverie whose end is just beginning.

MONK

Neither drunkenness nor chance nor the hammer
of the hand; not the search for notes between the notes,

the lost between the ivories like a fallen pair of keys;
not the demolition of a system; no need to dig, to make

this earth worth digging and therefore digging toward.
What you hear is its own argument for being. The laying

down of explanation's burden in the bricks of e-flat minor.
And if the clash is one more stone through the window,

if the major seven tonic comes crowned in shattered fragments,
it is—in spite of shock or rhetoric of ruin—a fortunate thing.

What you hear when notes get close is a waver not a wave.
Its pitches converse, unconverted, in ways the O's of ancient

choirs suppress. Thus the pathos of the not yet as it passes,
stained glass of the sun come crashing through the saint.

It comforts. It casts. It confuses. It spins the sharp
and brightly cornered style of the cue ball or the joke.

The hand that strikes is stricken. It needs a plume of dust
the way strings need tension, or the body a difficult night

to open what it must. I want to say the pain is in there,
and no sooner the black lid gapes. The harp beneath it rises.

The license board fires you again, for no good reason.
The accentual surprise that shivers our drinks has never been

this serious, this generous with the promise it hands to us
in pieces. Because it understands. We are far too broken,

too close, and never close enough. If another's music thumps
the wall, understand: there is a world in there, asleep in a chair.

A lone cigarette sits burning in a dish. The crack in the wall,
it is never coming out. Not as the lovely evidence it was.

The whole scene tells. Be patient as the plaster. Be
the air that takes and takes whatever blow the air imagines.

BLACKBIRD

Among those who travel freely in heaven and in hell,
Eric Dolphy's sax had the most magnanimous reach.

His breath swept from low to high the figures of a speech
so new to earth they asked, what is heaven if not this.

What is music if not a field in whom the lion lies down
with a lamb that one day is his sacrament. By nature.

What is a field if not a shatter, or the thousand pieces
if not a single flock once more. Every adolescent knows

the voice is born to break at the awkward age. That said,
the greater hell is none at all. No furnace of the sun

to forge the trumpet. No angel harp, no bee. No whimper
of the door that comes to us in memory and lets us enter.

No Eric Dophy whose voice strays across the threshold
to draw the animal from the anima, the good black milk

from the constellation. There is a forgotten world.
And one day, says the saxophone, *it will be heard, loved,*

invented. The sound of the wounded beast will bleed.
Its voice so desperately inflected, it will come to the edge

of a late night conversation and ask to be admitted.
And why not. What is a language without the unfamiliar term.

Or a thing so familiar you heard no music and then
you did. A cry so mournful and ecstatic in a pool of light

that needs the cold context of obscurity to shine.
It needs a measure of withholding in the rhythm section

to give the glass a frame. This voice in the hallway
between a music and what a music might become,

it needs to raise a question, a rebel sweetness in its
temperament, to shape the sure swift breath of a man

who knows a thing about a margin; he played like no one.
And no one saw he would die that night, so young.

Doctors would look at him, another dark musician,
and figure he is drugged, and by neglect destroy him.

No one shone a penlight in his eyes to see the tiny
constellations, the chilled light of musical angles

longing to be seen, named, unnamed to be seen again.
No one diagnosed the problem. No one tried.

Tonight the smoke of his body at the threshold gets
more tender the more I listen. In a rapture in a minor,

a wall begins to buckle like a lover at the knees.
Rafters shiver. Locks unpin their lions and their stars.

Heaven is a shattered thing. It says, *I too am invisible.*
I am not anger, not as you know it, see it, but the x-ray

of its want and error, bearing the torch of a nameless soul.
And yes, he played like no one. And no one released

the ghost in him, and the gates of paradise their thunder
and bronze, and the new red brass its thousand voices.

STRANGER

When I was young, I dialed a guitarist
	I had not seen in months, a gifted boy, quiet,

private, and his mother asked if I was a friend.
	I was, I thought, and then her voice broke

the odd sad news, and yes, I knew him,
	briefly. In the final days, we played his music.

I knew by his absence in class something was
	wrong—a better friend told me I should visit—

but I chose to know no more and so closed off
	my better self in a vaguely worried tune.

I would forgive most any kid more quickly
	than myself, and that difference dials its own

child where he sleeps. But beyond whatever
	shame, whatever invitation to the suffering

of another, I keep hearing in his mother's voice
the place he laid his beauty. *I am so sorry,*

I told her. And a part of me was talking to him.
A part is out there, sorry still, and listening.

When I was young, I learned there are birds
who make no song, pigeons who coo, at best,

and lift their wings to feed the young their milk.
Today is all a song to me. Which says, the art

is listening. Words, words, in each the dissonance
that inches toward some precipice of silence.

When I was sick and small, I was a stranger to myself,
and in that stranger a room with a phone,

and in that phone a bell and one bell-tone.
The tinier the bird the more rapidly it breathes.

The smaller the phone, the more terrible and small
the *here I am,* trilled so long as I refuse to answer.

CLOUD CHAMBER

For Harry Partch

The bells of the cloud chamber articulate in song
a temperament made of small and smaller pieces,

forty-three per octave and near impossible to sing,
and yet *natural,* as their composer conceived them,

for what you hear is always there, in the unfamiliar
sequence of tones inside of tones inside the voices

everywhere. Take any bell, any over-tonal tower
and tip it over. Such is the dream of the tower after all.

To lie low once again. To return to earth the angels
of its glass. Such is the language of a maker who,

having burned his opus in the even tempered modes,
aligned the new so close to common speech it entered

music as a stranger. It walked the way a cloud
walks across a mountain, and suddenly there is rain

in the kettle, a cricket in the blanket, and in the political
back and forth of homeless men the wanderer he was.

The bells here ring at intervals so peculiar to shatter one
is to find no other. And if he said, *no matter,* he was

talking to himself, wasted as a prince and unpretentious.
If he lapsed some nights into a blindness, nearly frozen

to extinction, he kept a notebook nonetheless. He slept
with it beneath the bridge that made his music large.

Times were tough and drunk. And on a good day,
they were drunker. If you strike a bell hard enough,

it drifts off key. Call it a cloud chamber then. Call it
conflicted. Call a body cold and the breath turns white.

Not as angels are, but the white of chalk the custodian
beats from the eraser. The white of rice in showers,

brides in clouds of lace and laughter falling into silk.
The pallor of these sheets, they know us. They accept.

In sickness and in health. The innocence of paper, it gives
its innocence away. Call it mercy, sweet ruinous desire.

For he will raise more clouds. And if you ask him what
five words are cruelest, he will tell you: *Go and sin no more.*

ZITHER

In a Ferris wheel overlooking the scaffolds
of postwar bewilderment and disrepair,

the star of our movie accentuates the word
victim as one might, in film, the authoritative

deformity or scar, when Lime, also known
as impossible Orson Wells, played by doubles

in long-shot overcoats and sewers until now,
considers the dots, also known as people

on the ground. How little it would mean
if one, he says, *stopped moving, forever.*

But nothing stops. What we see below is dirt
and shovels that turn it over without end,

digging out some basement garage or bomb
shelter for another movie, another war,

beyond the boom-chick and whimper
        of the zither, the café anthem of Viennese

distraction that moves men scene to scene,
        through the sewage and thrill rides of a fair

that cares for no one. It makes for a stronger
        entrance, this music that brings each friend-

turned-antagonist to meet us at the midway,
        his smile sharpened into someone who knows

the art of looking away, which is, these days,
        the art of looking everywhere behind you.

Every shadow the coat of a taller person.
        These days, the smart money is on zithers

whose sales soar, given their newly forged
        alliance in the drama, their home among

the scarred facades and sentimental waltzes.
        But instruments of innocence are hard.

Practice forever, and you still might hear
        a sizzling wire, a stutter of attack, a strain.

Which is what you tell your exhausted neighbor
when he pounds the wall to make you stop.

And you were just about to get somewhere,
to a Danube of wine bars and unfamiliar

faces; you were just about to take a table
inside the hundred candles, the angel dust

of black-market medications in your eyes.
Practice forever, and the world could turn

into a portico, the rubble to a backdrop,
the mood to a question like *what is the name*

of this song anyway. And why so somber.
You could find yourself trying to forget some

one, about to take a sip, when the glass tips
and shatters. The cloth goes red. Just you,

inexplicably in tears, searching for a waiter,
when you feel a hand on your sleeve—a stranger—

and, without thinking, you kneel down, together,
and cup the broken embers in your palms.

BACH

Bach died from 1750 to the present.
I read, and doubtless it is true, the dead

are dying still, and still dead, still their
music dies, becoming music after all.

And who here cannot recall the words
of every tune they loved, and love, who

has never made some up to voice what
we lost, and lose, to each mistaken song.

THE ARCTIC VARIATIONS

Dear earth, I too am turning pages of a requiem
        to all I see that is, as yet, unfinished.

Today a silence walks our campus, sun descends,
        the light of each lies down in its vessel,

where you appear, dear dark, a deeper fathom
        of the sky, greater than my measure

of you, ever smaller the details and never small
        enough. Students move their eyes

across their scores, and the beam that passes
        through moves some *thing*, some *one*,

though where we move grows ever more uncertain.
        What I do know is this. Somewhere

the oldest cliffs are coming down in sheets
        where a man on an ice floe plays piano.

I have seen it, and its voice spilled over the sills
of rooms where I am always a little

behind the news, always lost where the last
word turns to water. Somewhere a cliff

gives beneath the pressure of the sun,
a black fathom rises from the ocean floor,

and the music that you hear is the warmest year
on record. I learned that today.

My fact eaten by the other facts in the long
evolutionary chain of truths and negotiations

struggling to survive. Oceans rise, billow.
Soon a nuclear snow, if it snows, will

torch the field to ashes. Last night a blaze
of red spread across my nation's map.

And I, confused, blew smoke from the surface.
I blew a wish from the weary candle,

and asked where did it go. *So you think you
are better than me?* said the smoke.

Or was that me, my solitary nation, my map

        that is an angry god eating the last of the facts.

Dear death, I wish you were alive. Here

        in my idea of you, in the meadowlands

of words and tropes whose mouths are filled

        with earth. What I know I know is this.

Long ago my father leaned against the rail

        of a world war cruiser lost in the Sea of Japan.

When I see my nation, I see this. I see a distant

        detail among the other details of the planet.

And the music is enormous, frightening in its beauty,

        ablaze at dusk. I too have sworn allegiance

to a red thing hung in the corner and grown afraid.

        I have gazed at the heads of presidents

on classroom walls and thought, how dull to maintain

        your one sententious stare, wall after wall.

Serious as the mountain face that no one scales alive.

        Dear childhood, I have seen your ocean.

I have heard your waves beside my bed, and no sooner
	sleepers arrive with their pillows and pills,

their Bibles and soft synthetic sheep. I want
	to tell them a story that says we all come from

the same blood, the wine of the fathoms, same
	sea that rises and moves against a native shore.

Boundaries breathe. Like us. They must.
	When a soldier dies, he holds a door open.

When he drowns, he leads us to a meadow of waves.
	I have heard the bronze peroration touch

the widowed hand. Dear ice, when I think of you,
	I think of this. I see you as a place just north

of north. When I think of life after life, a planetary
	furnace blows a phantom through the ocean

floor. Hell, life is hard in the middle. I know.
	You wake up in the dark, fry eggs, boil coffee,

feed the beasts that grace the tables of the coast.
	You shovel a stench as corrosive as the dawn

that breaks across the stockyard. Your hands
are not your hands. They are maps.

And when a map says, *so you think you are better*
than me, I tell myself, be clear. It is a map.

Not earth. It is an abstract in a way that music
cannot be, having laid its argument down in

the water. When the winds come and the cliff
face trembles, Earth is always a step ahead,

as music is and what it burns, always slightly ahead
of itself, and yet there it is, in the man

and the piano and the soft white breath, the legs
beneath the burden lodged in ice, to each its

deepening print—no, deeper—as graves are deep
in conversation. And in the dissonance you hear.

ACKNOWLEDGMENTS

The author would like to thank the following publications in which this poetry has previously appeared: *Asheville Poetry Review, Blackbird, Brilliant Corners, The Common, Georgia Review, The Literary Review, Michigan Quarterly Review, Narrative, Plume, Poetry, Prairie Schooner, Southwest Review, Solstice, SplitLevel Journal,* and *Yale Review.* The poem "Bells" appeared in *Best American Poetry 2020.*